調和 Chōwa: Japan's Dance with Innovation

By Yoshida Yuki

Table of Contents

Introduction: The Bamboo and the Microchip
Where tradition and technology meet in modern Japan

Chapter 1: The Art of Creative Preservation
How Japanese culture maintains tradition by constantly reinventing it

Chapter 2: The Innovation of Craft
From sword-making to robotics: the continuity of Japanese craftsmanship

Chapter 3: The Taste of Time
Culinary traditions and innovations that define Japanese identity

Chapter 4: Synthetic Humanity
Robots, AI, and the Japanese vision of technological harmony

Chapter 5: The Business of Continuity
Family companies and corporate longevity in Japanese commerce

Chapter 6: Animated Ancestors
How popular culture preserves ancient stories in new forms

Chapter 7: Kami in the Machine
Spiritual traditions in Japan's technological landscape

Chapter 8: Forest and Concrete
Urban planning and architecture as expressions of tradition and modernity

Chapter 9: Wrapped Meanings
How aesthetics of packaging reveal Japan's approach to both old and new

Chapter 10: The Rhythm of Reinvention
Seasonal awareness and Japan's unique relationship with change

Chapter 11: Fracturing and Mending
Kintsugi philosophy in Japan's response to disaster and change

Chapter 12: Seeds of the Future
Educational approaches that balance tradition and innovation

Conclusion: The Space Between
Lessons from Japan for a world in transition

Introduction: The Bamboo and the Microchip

The first time my American mother tried to throw away a perfectly good chopstick wrapper, my father nearly had a heart attack.

"Mottainai!" he exclaimed, snatching it from her hand. With meticulous care, he folded the paper into an origami crane, placed it beside his plate, and continued eating as if nothing unusual had happened.

My mother looked at me, bewildered. I shrugged, caught between worlds as usual.

That evening, I found the paper crane perched on my pillow. When I asked my father about it the next morning, he simply said, "Yesterday's wrapper, today's art, tomorrow's memory." Then he winked and returned to his newspaper.

Growing up half-Japanese in Kyoto during the technology boom of the 1980s, these small cultural collisions were my daily bread. My American mother valued efficiency and practicality; my Japanese father saw poetry in mundane objects and ritual in everyday actions. Their marriage was itself a dance between different worlds—much like Japan itself.

When I was seven, my grandfather began taking me to the bamboo forests at the edge of Kyoto. "Look carefully," he would say, pointing to the tall green stalks that seemed to touch the sky. "Bamboo teaches us everything we need to know about Japan."

I remember running my small fingers along the jointed stem, feeling the rings that marked years of growth. "Bamboo bends but never breaks," he explained. "It honors its roots while reaching toward heaven."

"There's a word for this," he added. "Chōwa (調和)."

"What does it mean?" I asked.

"Harmony. Balance. The peaceful coexistence of different elements." He gestured toward where the bamboo met the sky. "Not compromise where each side gives something up, but true integration where each element remains fully itself while creating something greater together."

This concept—chōwa—would become my framework for understanding Japan. Unlike the Western tendency to see tradition and innovation as opposing forces, chōwa suggests they can exist in harmonious relationship, each strengthening rather than diminishing the other. This isn't just philosophical abstraction but a practical approach visible throughout Japanese culture—from architecture and craftsmanship to business and technology.

Thirty years later, I find myself in Tokyo's Akihabara district, watching a robot delicately serve coffee to a table of foreign tourists. The machine bows slightly—an unnecessary flourish programmed by someone who understood that in Japan, even robots need proper manners. Nearby, young programmers huddle over laptops, developing AI algorithms that might power the next generation of mechanical servants.

The tourists snap photos, delighted by what they see as a novelty. But I still hear my grandfather's words echoing across decades. The bamboo and the microchip—ancient wisdom and cutting-edge technology—are not opponents in some cultural tug-of-war. They are dance partners in the continuing story of Japan. They exemplify chōwa.

"Only in Japan," I mutter to myself, as the robot carefully adjusts a crooked saucer with the same precision a tea ceremony master might employ.

A nearby programmer overhears me and laughs. "My grandmother would scold that robot for improper form," he says in Japanese. When I reply in kind, his eyes widen with surprise at finding a "foreigner" who speaks like a native. I don't bother explaining my mixed heritage—another conversation for another day.

This book is my attempt, after twenty years of chronicling Japanese culture for Western audiences (and being mistaken for a tourist in my father's homeland), to explain perhaps the most fascinating paradox of Japan: how a society so deeply reverent of its past has simultaneously become one of the world's most innovative nations. This is not a simple tale of tradition versus progress, but rather a complex dance between preservation and reinvention that has shaped Japan's unique place in the global conversation.

As you journey through these pages, I invite you to set aside Western binary thinking that places tradition and innovation in opposition. In Japan, they achieve chōwa—harmony through integration rather than compromise. To understand this balance is to gain insight not just into Japan, but into one of the fundamental challenges facing all modern societies: how to move forward without losing our souls.

In each chapter, we'll explore a different aspect of this dance—from architecture and craftsmanship to food and technology—seeing how Japan maintains continuity with its past while embracing necessary change. I'll share personal experiences and conversations with masters, innovators, and ordinary people who live at the intersection of ancient wisdom and cutting-edge technology.

While my focus will primarily be on the elegant achievements of this balance, I won't shy away from examining the challenges that test it. Japan's aging population, gender inequality, work-life imbalances, and economic stagnation all strain the harmony between old and new. These challenges reveal that chōwa is not a static achievement but a dynamic process requiring continuous adjustment and renewal.

Welcome to the space between worlds. Let's explore together.

Chapter 1: The Art of Creative Preservation

The Living Shrine

"You came all this way to watch people take apart a building?"

The American tourist next to me looks genuinely confused as we stand in the autumn chill at Ise, watching white-robed Shinto priests methodically dismantle Japan's most sacred shrine. His wife checks her guidebook, evidently wondering if they've made a scheduling error.

I smile. "It's like watching your grandmother make a recipe she's cooked for sixty years without writing it down. The value isn't just in eating the food but in seeing how the knowledge passes from one generation to the next."

The man looks unconvinced, but stays anyway, his camera hanging unused around his neck as ancient timbers—some weighing several tons—are carefully removed from the simple yet elegant structure.

What we're witnessing is not destruction but one of Japan's most profound acts of preservation: the ceremony of *shikinen sengu*, a tradition that has continued for over 1,300 years. Every twenty years, this shrine is completely rebuilt on an adjacent plot of land—a perpetual cycle of death and rebirth that has outlasted empires.

Every twenty years, the Ise Grand Shrine is completely rebuilt on an adjacent plot of land. New materials replicate the ancient design with exacting precision, using traditional tools and techniques. No nails pierce the precious hinoki cypress wood; instead, complex joinery techniques lock everything into place. When complete, the divine presence—the sacred mirror representing the sun goddess Amaterasu—is transferred to its new home, and the cycle begins again.

To Western eyes, this might seem a curious paradox. Is the shrine 1,300 years old, or just twenty? The question reveals a fundamental difference in how cultures perceive preservation. While the West often preserves by preventing change—keeping original materials intact in museums and historical sites—Japan frequently preserves through controlled renewal.

"We do not preserve the building," explains Takashi Mori, one of the shrine's caretakers. "We preserve the knowledge of how to build it. The form remains perfectly consistent, but the material is always new."

This approach—what I call creative preservation—appears throughout Japanese culture. Ancient temples are carefully dismantled and reconstructed using traditional methods. Master craftsmen pass down techniques through apprenticeship systems, ensuring that ancient arts remain viable in contemporary contexts. Kabuki theater maintains historical forms while subtly incorporating modern sensibilities.

In Japanese thinking, impermanence (*mujō*) is not something to be defeated but accepted as the natural order. Preservation efforts focus not on stopping time but on maintaining the knowledge, skills, and aesthetic principles that give cultural treasures their meaning. The result is a living tradition rather than a fossilized one.

By the time the ceremony concludes, the American tourist is furiously taking notes instead of photos. "This is blowing my mind," he tells me. "In America, we'd put a climate-controlled glass box around the original and call it preserved."

I laugh. "Then you'd have a dead shrine instead of a living one. The priests here would find that far more destructive than what we just watched."

Later, as we part ways, he thanks me for the explanation. "I came to Japan expecting to see a lot of old stuff," he says. "I didn't expect to completely rethink what 'old' actually means."

The Constant Within Change

This philosophy extends beyond architecture and arts into daily life and industrial practices. Consider the humble bento box, a traditional packed meal dating back centuries. The basic concept remains consistent—a portable, balanced meal in compartmentalized containers—yet the form constantly evolves. Modern bento boxes might feature vacuum insulation, sophisticated locking mechanisms, or character designs from popular anime, while maintaining the essential principles of variety, balance, and visual appeal that defined the earliest bento.

Japanese companies often approach innovation similarly, maintaining core traditions while embracing transformation. Toyota's production systems revolutionized global manufacturing while drawing explicitly on traditional Japanese concepts like *kaizen* (continuous improvement). Nintendo began as a playing card company in 1889 before evolving into a global technology giant, yet still maintains a distinctly Japanese approach to entertainment that emphasizes playful interaction over pure technology.

"We are not interested in technology for its own sake," Shigeru Miyamoto, Nintendo's legendary game designer, once told me during an interview in Kyoto. "The technology must serve the experience, the joy of play. This philosophy hasn't changed since we made cards for family games over a century ago."

This tension—between reverence for the past and openness to transformation—creates a distinctive innovative environment. Japanese creativity often thrives not through revolutionary breaks with tradition but through evolutionary adaptations that maintain cultural continuity while embracing new possibilities.

As I watched the dismantling of Ise Shrine, I realized I was witnessing not just a religious ceremony but a master class in Japanese cultural psychology. The shrine embodies a profound cultural insight: that preservation and renewal are not opposing forces but complementary processes. To truly preserve something meaningful, you must allow it to be reborn.

Chapter 2: The Innovation of Craft

The Sword and the Robot

"Please don't touch anything," says Master swordsmith Gassan Sadatoshi without looking up from his forge. "The American journalist before you burned his hand and then dropped my hammer on his foot. I had to sweep up broken camera parts for days."

I freeze mid-step, my hand hovering near a rack of tools whose purpose I can only guess at. How did he know? His back was turned to me the entire time.

"You breathe like someone about to touch something expensive," he explains, still focused on the glowing steel before him. "Twenty-two generations of swordsmiths in my family. We develop certain... intuitions."

I laugh nervously and tuck my hands safely into my pockets. For the next three hours, I watch in silence as Gassan-sensei performs a dance virtually unchanged for a millennium. His movements are methodical, almost meditative, as he folds a piece of steel again and again, building up thousands of microscopic layers. Over the next several months, this humble metal will become a katana of exceptional quality—a Japanese sword that stands among the world's greatest achievements in metallurgy.

"You're staring at my hands but should be watching the steel," he says suddenly. "The steel tells me what it needs. I am merely its servant."

The next day finds me thirty miles away in Osaka, watching robots assemble the latest generation of semiconductor chips in a sterile manufacturing facility. I'm suited head-to-toe in clean room gear that makes me look like a character from a science fiction film. My guide, Dr. Tanaka, leads me along a catwalk above the factory floor.

"Our tolerances are measured in nanometers," she explains proudly. "A human hair is about 80,000 nanometers thick. Our machines work with precisions of 5 nanometers."

Below us, robotic arms move with balletic precision, assembling components that will power artificial intelligence systems capable of learning and adapting to their environments. The room hums with the sound of filtered air and servo motors.

"Impressive," I say, "but completely different from what I saw yesterday."

Dr. Tanaka raises an eyebrow. "Where were you yesterday?"

"Watching Gassan Sadatoshi forge a sword in Kyoto."

She smiles broadly. "Ah! My father collects his works. Did you know our head engineer visits his workshop every year?"

These two scenes—the ancient swordsmith and the modern robotics factory—might seem worlds apart to Western observers. Yet in the Japanese context, they represent not a rupture but a continuity. The philosophical approach that guides Gassan-sensei's hand can be found, transmuted but recognizable, in the clean rooms of Japan's most advanced technology companies.

"Our robots are calibrated by master technicians who train for a decade before they're allowed to work on the most sensitive equipment," Dr. Tanaka continues. "They develop what we call 'finger wisdom'—a sensitivity beyond what instruments can measure." She laughs. "Very similar to your swordsmith, no?"

The Soul in the Object

To understand this continuity, we must recognize how differently craftsmanship is conceptualized in Japanese culture. The Western tradition tends to separate the functional and spiritual aspects of creation—a sword is a weapon, a tool with practical purpose. In the Japanese tradition, particularly as influenced by Shinto animism, objects possess spirit (*kami*). The craftsman's role is not merely to shape material but to reveal or enhance this inherent spiritual quality.

"I am not creating the sword," Gassan-sensei explained to me as he demonstrated his technique. "I am helping the steel become what it already wishes to be."

This philosophy—that materials have inherent properties and desires that the craftsman must respect—appears in virtually all traditional Japanese crafts. Pottery masters speak of "listening" to the clay. Woodworkers describe "releasing" the forms hidden within the grain. Paper makers attune themselves to the subtle qualities of plant fibers.

The technical results of this approach are remarkable. Japanese traditional crafts achieve extraordinary functionality through deep material understanding rather than through brute-force technological solutions. The katana's legendary cutting ability comes not from being the hardest steel but from an ingenious composite structure that balances hardness and flexibility. Traditional Japanese carpentry creates earthquake-resistant structures without nails or screws, using joinery that allows buildings to flex rather than shatter during seismic events.

From Craft to Technology

When Japan began rapid industrialization in the Meiji era (1868-1912), many observers predicted that traditional craftsmanship would disappear, replaced by Western-style mass production. Instead, something more interesting happened: craft values migrated into industrial contexts, creating a distinctly Japanese approach to manufacturing and technology development.

Consider the case of Toyota's production system, now studied worldwide. When Taiichi Ohno and Eiji Toyoda developed the Toyota Production System in the 1950s and 60s, they incorporated traditional craft concepts in surprising ways. The emphasis on eliminating waste (*muda*) echoes the efficiency of traditional Japanese packaging. The concept of *jidoka*—automation with a human touch—maintains the craftsman's oversight within mechanized processes. Most importantly, Toyota's famous quality circles applied the master-apprentice knowledge-sharing model to industrial contexts.

I witnessed this philosophical continuity firsthand while visiting a semiconductor factory in Kumamoto. The clean room supervisor, Tanaka-san, described his team's approach to maintaining the complex lithography equipment:

"Each machine has its own character, its own spirit," he told me through a translator. "Our best technicians can tell what is wrong just by listening to the sound it makes, like a doctor with a stethoscope. We teach younger workers to develop this sensitivity—to know the machine not just through data but through all their senses."

This language—virtually identical to what I'd heard from traditional craftsmen—reveals how deeply craft thinking has penetrated even the most advanced technological enterprises in Japan.

The New Craftsmen

Perhaps nowhere is this continuity more evident than in Japan's robotics industry. While Western approaches to robotics often emphasize replacing human capabilities, Japanese robotics frequently focus on augmenting and extending them.

At Tokyo University's JSK Laboratory, I observed engineers developing robotic exoskeletons designed to help elderly craftspeople continue their work despite physical limitations. Rather than replacing the master carpenter or weaver, these systems preserve their knowledge and skills by overcoming bodily constraints.

"The robot is not the craftsman," explained Dr. Nakamura, the lab director. "It is the craftsman's new hands. The knowledge, the sensitivity, the judgment—these remain human. We are not trying to teach robots to replace these masters but to serve them, to become extensions of their will."

This approach reflects Japan's distinctive relationship with technology—not as a replacement for tradition but as a new medium through which traditional values and approaches can find expression. From Nintendo's digital games that emphasize the traditional value of social play to textile companies integrating traditional patterns into high-tech fabrics, Japanese innovation often functions as a vehicle for cultural continuity rather than disruption.

As Gassan-sensei completes another fold in his sword steel, the metal glowing orange in the dimness of his workshop, he embodies a philosophy that continues to shape Japan's approach to creation—whether the medium is ancient steel or quantum computing. The hand changes, but the spirit remains.

Chapter 3: The Taste of Time

The Memory of Flavor

My American cousin visits Japan for the first time and insists on eating at McDonald's.

"We came halfway across the world," I protest, "and you want the same burger you eat at home?"

"I'm curious," he defends himself. "Japanese McDonald's is supposed to be different."

Reluctantly, I take him to the golden arches in Shibuya. He orders a Teriyaki McBurger, ebi (shrimp) filet, and green tea McFlurry—none of which exist in American branches. He's delighted by the differences and spends fifteen minutes photographing his meal from every angle.

"See?" he says triumphantly. "Even your fast food tells a story about adapting while maintaining identity."

I concede the point but extract a promise: tomorrow we'll experience the other end of the culinary timeline.

The next day, the first thing that strikes us about Honke Owariya in Kyoto is not what has changed, but what hasn't. Founded in 1465—before Columbus reached America—this soba restaurant has served handmade buckwheat noodles for over 25 generations. The current owner, Ryusuke Nakamura, represents the 16th generation of his family to run the establishment.

"I'm disappointed," my cousin whispers as we remove our shoes. "I expected something more... impressive for a place this old."

I smile knowingly. "That's exactly the point."

"Our recipe hasn't changed in centuries," Nakamura-san tells us as we sit in the traditional tatami room upstairs. "The buckwheat is still stone-ground daily. The noodles are still cut by hand. Even the dipping sauce follows the same proportions."

My cousin nods politely, clearly still underwhelmed by the simple setting and food presentation. Then he takes his first bite.

His eyes widen. "This is just... noodles. How does it taste like... like..."

"Like the distilled essence of every satisfying meal you've ever had?" I suggest.

"Exactly!" He takes another bite, slower this time. "It's so simple but so complete."

Nakamura-san smiles at the familiar reaction. "The emperor himself has eaten our soba," he says modestly. "We served the Imperial household for generations."

Yet despite this apparent conservatism, Owariya has not remained static. As we finish our meal, Nakamura-san shows us their new offerings: gluten-free options alongside traditional fare, famous soba-boro cookies that ship worldwide through an e-commerce site, and a photo of their branch location in a Kyoto department store that serves commuters with limited time.

My cousin points to an iPad behind the counter. "For a place that's been around since the 1400s, you seem pretty comfortable with technology."

Nakamura-san laughs. "The chopsticks evolved from twigs, but they still serve their purpose. Technology is just another set of chopsticks."

As we leave, we're greeted by a young woman in a business suit who introduces herself as Nakamura Yui, the owner's daughter and future successor of the restaurant.

"You're the next generation?" my cousin asks. "Is that... unusual for a woman in Japan?"

She smiles diplomatically. "Traditionally, yes. But traditions evolve. I studied business at Keio University and worked at a tech company before returning here. My father believes my experience with both modern business practices and traditional culinary arts is exactly what Owariya needs for its next century."

My cousin looks impressed. "In America, we'd call that having the best of both worlds."

"In Japan," she replies, "we call it necessary. Our challenge isn't choosing between tradition and innovation, but finding how they support each other."

Later, I learn that Yui-san represents a growing trend. While Japanese business succession has historically favored male heirs, economic pressures and changing social attitudes have opened new pathways for women. Many traditional businesses now embrace female leadership, finding that women often excel at the delicate balance between preserving core traditions and adapting to contemporary markets.

This balance—maintaining the essential while adapting the peripheral—characterizes Japan's approach to culinary tradition. Unlike some food cultures that resist change in the name of authenticity, Japanese cuisine has continuously evolved while maintaining distinctive aesthetic and philosophical principles.

The Five Principles

To understand this evolution, we must recognize the core principles that define Japanese culinary tradition:

1. Seasonality (*shun*): The celebration of ingredients at their peak moment of perfection

2. Minimalism: The art of restraint, letting natural flavors speak without excessive manipulation

3. Balance: Not just of flavors but of textures, temperatures, and visual elements

4. Technique: Precision methods that enhance rather than mask an ingredient's essence

5. Presentation: The visual arrangement that engages all senses in the dining experience

These principles remain constant even as specific dishes and ingredients change. They create a framework flexible enough to incorporate new elements while maintaining cultural continuity.

Consider the evolution of sushi. This quintessentially Japanese dish began as a preservation method—fish fermented with rice, with the rice typically discarded. Over centuries, it transformed into *narezushi* (partly fermented), then *hayazushi* (no fermentation), and finally *nigirizushi* (hand-pressed), the form most familiar internationally today.

Each iteration maintained core Japanese culinary values while adapting to changing circumstances. When refrigeration became available, sushi chefs didn't abandon tradition—they used the technology to expand possibilities while maintaining the principles of seasonality and peak flavor.

The New Traditional

This pattern continues in contemporary Japan, where culinary innovation often takes the form of applying traditional principles to new contexts rather than abandoning tradition entirely.

At Den in Tokyo, chef Zaiyu Hasegawa serves what appears at first glance to be traditional *kaiseki* cuisine—Japan's formal multi-course dining tradition. Look closer, however, and you notice surprising elements: a garden salad arranged like a living ecosystem, complete with edible "insects"; fried chicken served in a custom box mimicking fast-food packaging; dessert that requires diners to "dig" for hidden components.

"I'm not breaking tradition," Hasegawa explained when I dined there. "I'm continuing it. The principles—

seasonality, balance, technique—remain sacred. But each generation must find its own expression of these principles."

This approach appears throughout Japan's food landscape. Convenience stores offer onigiri (rice balls) with traditional fillings alongside innovative new combinations. Department store food halls preserve ancient confectionery arts while introducing contemporary flavors. Even chain restaurants typically maintain Japanese culinary aesthetics while streamlining production.

For foreign companies entering Japan's food market, this balance has proven challenging to navigate. Starbucks succeeded by developing Japan-specific items that honor local tastes—seasonal sakura lattes, matcha frappuccinos—while maintaining its core offerings. McDonald's struggled initially but found success after developing rice-based burgers and green tea desserts that acknowledged Japanese preferences.

The Future of Tradition

Japan's culinary future continues this dance between preservation and innovation. At the Kikkoman Research Laboratory in Noda, scientists study the molecular structures of traditional fermented foods like soy sauce and miso, not to replace traditional methods but to understand why they work so effectively.

"We are using science to explain what our ancestors discovered through centuries of careful observation," explained Dr. Kimura, the lab's director. "This doesn't replace traditional knowledge but helps us preserve it by understanding it more deeply."

This scientific approach has led to remarkable innovations that extend rather than disrupt tradition. Researchers have developed new soy sauce varieties with reduced sodium while maintaining traditional flavor profiles. Traditional fermentation techniques have inspired probiotic products that address contemporary health concerns. Ancient preservation methods have found new applications in modern convenience foods.

What makes this evolution distinctly Japanese is not just what changes but what remains constant. The aesthetic and philosophical framework—the reverence for seasonality, the celebration of minimalism, the attention to presentation—continues unbroken from imperial court cuisines to contemporary molecular gastronomy.

As I finish my meal at Owariya, savoring the distinctive nutty flavor of buckwheat noodles made as they have been for centuries, I realize that what I'm tasting is not just food but time itself—the accumulated wisdom of generations who understood that true innovation doesn't require abandoning tradition but reinventing it, continuously, with reverence and imagination.

Chapter 4: Synthetic Humanity

The Robot and the Child

"Pepper-kun is being weird again," announces five-year-old Yuki, hands on her hips as she addresses her kindergarten teacher. The other children nod in solemn agreement.

I glance at the small humanoid robot in the corner of the classroom in Kanagawa Prefecture. Pepper stands motionless, its large eyes dim.

The teacher approaches the robot and checks a panel on its back. "The battery needs charging," she explains. "Shall we plug Pepper-kun in for his nap?"

The children chorus "Hai!" and watch attentively as their mechanical classmate is connected to a charging station. One boy pats the robot's head. "Good night, Pepper-kun. Get strong again."

I expected many things when visiting a Japanese kindergarten with a robot teaching assistant, but this casual tenderness wasn't one of them. When Pepper reactivates an hour later, the children welcome it back with the same natural warmth they would show a returning friend. They speak to it naturally, laugh at its jokes, and gently correct it when it makes mistakes. When one child becomes frustrated with a drawing, Pepper offers encouragement in a soothing voice. The child nods and returns to the task.

"In America, would children treat the robot this way?" asks the principal, who has been quietly observing my reactions.

"I think American children would either be afraid of it or try to break it," I admit. "They wouldn't speak to it like a person with feelings."

She nods thoughtfully. "Here, everything has a spirit—mountains, rivers, old temple bells… why not robots too?"

This scene—robots as natural companions rather than threatening others—reflects a distinctly Japanese comfort with artificial beings that has deep cultural roots. While Western narratives often frame artificial intelligence and robotics as existential threats (from Frankenstein to The Terminator), Japanese cultural traditions have long been more accommodating to the idea that humanity and artificial beings might coexist harmoniously.

The Animated World

To understand this difference, we must recognize how Shinto traditions have shaped Japanese perceptions of consciousness and spirit. In Shinto animism, consciousness is not exclusively human—mountains, rivers, trees, and even human-made objects can possess *kami* (spirit). The boundaries between the animate and inanimate, the natural and artificial, have always been more permeable in Japanese cultural imagination.

Japanese folklore abounds with stories of objects gaining consciousness. The *tsukumogami* tales describe household items that come alive after one hundred years of service. Far from being horror stories, these narratives often portray such transformations as natural progressions rather than violations of cosmic order.

"In Western thought, creating artificial life often represents hubris—humans overstepping their boundaries," explains Professor Hiroshi Ishiguro, the renowned roboticist from Osaka University. "In Japanese tradition, bringing objects to life can be seen as recognizing the spirit that already exists within them."

This cultural foundation helps explain Japan's distinctive approach to robotics and artificial intelligence. Rather than asking whether machines can or should replicate human capabilities, Japanese developers have often focused on how machines and humans might form new kinds of relationships.

The Mechanical Garden

At Toyota's Robotics Research Institute in Toyota City, engineers are developing care robots designed to assist Japan's rapidly aging population. Unlike Western approaches that often emphasize full automation to replace human caregivers, these systems are explicitly designed to support rather than replace human care networks.

"The robot is not a substitute for human connection," explains lead engineer Matsumoto Hiroshi. "It is a tool that makes human connection more possible by handling routine tasks so that family members and professional caregivers can focus on the emotional and social aspects of care."

This philosophy extends beyond elder care into various domains. Japan's industrial robots are frequently designed to work alongside human workers rather than completely replacing them. Educational robots supplement rather than substitute for human teachers. Even entertainment robots like Sony's Aibo are designed primarily to enhance human relationships rather than replace them.

This collaborative approach reflects a distinctly Japanese understanding of the relationship between tradition and innovation—not as competing forces but as complementary energies that can be harmonized.

The Human in the Machine

Perhaps the most fascinating aspect of Japan's approach to artificial intelligence is how it has preserved traditional concepts of harmony, mindfulness, and social connection within these new technologies.

At the Riken Institute's Guardian Robot Project, researchers are developing robots with sophisticated emotional intelligence capabilities. These systems are programmed not just to perform tasks but to do so with awareness of human emotional states and social contexts.

"The traditional Japanese concept of *kikubari*—the ability to anticipate others' needs without explicit communication—is central to our design philosophy," explains project director Dr. Minoru Asada. "We're teaching our systems to read subtle cues, to understand context, to move gracefully in human spaces—principles that come directly from traditional Japanese social values."

This approach stands in stark contrast to approaches that treat AI primarily as a means of processing massive datasets or optimizing for efficiency. The Japanese vision often emphasizes qualities like considerateness, contextual awareness, and social harmony—values deeply embedded in traditional culture.

Even in popular culture, Japan has explored human-AI relationships with distinctive nuance. From Astro Boy (created in 1952) to contemporary anime like "Time of Eve," Japanese stories frequently portray robots developing emotions, moral reasoning, and meaningful relationships with humans. These narratives rarely frame such developments as threatening or unnatural, instead exploring the potential for new kinds of connection and understanding.

The Harmonious Future

As global debates about AI ethics intensify, Japan's distinctive approach offers valuable perspective. Rather than focusing primarily on preventing harm or maintaining human control—though these concerns are certainly present—Japanese frameworks often emphasize creating harmonious relationships between humans and intelligent systems.

The government's "Society 5.0" initiative explicitly articulates this vision, describing a future where digital transformation enhances rather than disrupts traditional social values. The goal is not technological advancement for its own sake but the creation of a "super-smart society" that uses technology to support human flourishing within established cultural frameworks.

"We are not seeking to create a new world," explains Cabinet Secretary Yoshimasa Hayashi. "We are seeking to create new tools that allow us to better express the values our culture has always cherished—harmony, consideration for others, respect for elders, connection to nature."

As I watch the kindergarteners interact with Pepper, I'm struck by how naturally they accept this mechanical entity as part of their social world. There is no fear, no sense of categorical difference—just another being with whom they can interact, learn, and grow.

This acceptance reflects a profound cultural insight: that the boundary between human and non-human, natural and artificial, is not fixed but fluid. Innovation need not threaten tradition; properly conceived, it can become a vehicle through which traditional values find new expression in a changing world.

In this way, Japan's robots embody not a break with the past but a continuation of it—a new verse in an ancient song about what it means to exist in a world where spirit moves through all things, even those we ourselves create.

Chapter 5: The Business of Continuity

The Century Club

"You're telling me this shop has been making the same sweet for a thousand years? That's... impossible." My friend Dave, visiting from Silicon Valley, stands outside Ichiwa with the skeptical expression of a man who measures success in quarterly reports and product launches.

"Not just the same sweet," I explain, "but in the same location, by the same family. Twenty-five generations of making *aburi-mochi* exactly the same way."

Dave peers through the modest wooden entrance. "In America, we'd have franchised it, changed the recipe to improve margins, expanded internationally, and eventually sold to a conglomerate."

"And that," I tell him as we duck into the small shop, "is exactly why you don't have thousand-year-old businesses."

Founded in 1000 CE, this humble enterprise on a quiet Kyoto street has survived wars, disasters, and dramatic social changes. The simple rice cakes they make—grilled mochi topped with sweet miso—haven't changed since the shop opened. Neither has their business model, location, or core philosophy.

After sampling the deceptively simple sweet, Dave falls uncharacteristically silent. "It tastes... timeless," he finally says. "Like something that should never change."

"That's the entire point," I reply.

Ichiwa is not an anomaly. Japan is home to over 33,000 businesses that have operated for more than a century, including over 3,100 that have existed for at least 200 years. The world's oldest continuously operating company—Kongō Gumi, a temple construction firm founded in 578 CE—operated independently for 1,428 years before becoming a subsidiary of a larger construction company in 2006.

This remarkable corporate longevity reveals something essential about Japan's approach to business: the company itself often matters more than immediate profit or individual success. The business becomes a vehicle for cultural continuity, maintaining traditions across generations while simultaneously adapting to changing circumstances.

"But what about economic growth?" Dave asks as we stroll through Kyoto's traditional shopping district. "Japan's been stagnant for decades while Silicon Valley created trillions in new value."

It's a fair question, and one that reveals the tension in Japan's business philosophy. The same values that create extraordinary stability—prioritizing continuity over expansion, quality over volume, relation over transaction—have contributed to Japan's economic challenges. Since the asset bubble burst in the early 1990s, Japan has experienced over three decades of low growth and deflation despite numerous stimulus attempts.

"It's not so black and white," I explain. "These traditional businesses aren't Japan's entire economy. They coexist with global powerhouses like Toyota, Sony, and Softbank that drive innovation and growth. The challenge for Japan's economy isn't eliminating these traditional businesses but finding the right balance—or chōwa—between stability and growth, preservation and innovation."

This economic duality mirrors Japan's broader cultural approach. While Germany has focused on industrial efficiency and the United States on rapid innovation, Japan has pursued a third path that integrates elements of both approaches while maintaining cultural distinctiveness. The result is an economy that produces both thousand-year-old confectionaries and cutting-edge robotics—sometimes within the same company.

"Japan's traditional businesses are stabilizers," I continue. "They provide economic resilience during downturns, maintain craft knowledge that might otherwise disappear, and preserve cultural identity amid globalization. They're not obstacles to growth but foundations for a different kind of prosperity—one measured in generational well-being rather than quarterly results."

Dave nods thoughtfully. "Still, something's got to give, right? Japan's population is shrinking, its debt is massive, and young people are struggling to find stable jobs. How sustainable is this system, really?"

"That's the trillion-yen question," I acknowledge. "Japan is facing unprecedented demographic challenges that test the limits of its traditional business model. But rather than abandoning its approach, it's trying to evolve it—finding ways to balance continuity with necessary change. Whether that will succeed remains to be seen."

Family and Legacy

At a traditional washi paper workshop in the mountains of Fukui Prefecture, I watch Tsuchiya Hisashi carefully examine a freshly made sheet of paper, holding it up to the light to check for imperfections. His hands—weathered and stained from decades of work—move with the precision that comes only from endless repetition.

"My daughter asks why I won't buy the new German papermaking equipment," he says with a chuckle. "It would triple our production overnight."

"And will you?" I ask.

He smiles, the corners of his eyes crinkling. "When you inherit a business that has survived for centuries, you think differently about time. I am not just running a business; I am preserving a legacy that will outlive me. My responsibility is not only to today's customers and employees but to future generations who will carry this knowledge forward."

As the 16th-generation owner of a traditional papermaking company founded in 1595, Tsuchiya-san embodies a perspective that shapes Japanese business practices in distinctive ways. Many long-established companies (*shinise*) maintain relatively modest profit targets, focusing instead on stable employment, consistent quality, and community relationships. They frequently limit expansion to protect core competencies and maintain hands-on quality control.

Later, over tea, I mention that his approach might seem conservative to Western business minds.

"We could certainly grow larger," he admits, tapping the delicate teacup with his still-damp fingers. "But expansion would require compromises in our production methods. We choose to stay small enough that every sheet of paper receives the attention it deserves."

He pauses, then adds with unexpected sharpness: "Is it conservative to want your great-grandchildren to have a business to inherit? In Japan, we build companies to last centuries, not to sell to the highest bidder after a few good quarters."

This conservative approach might seem at odds with innovation, yet these ancient companies have demonstrated remarkable adaptability. Toraya, a confectionery business founded in the early 16th century, still produces traditional Japanese sweets but now also creates modern versions with reduced sugar for health-conscious consumers. It has expanded into international markets while maintaining its core identity and production values.

The secret to this balance lies not in resisting change but in approaching it selectively and incrementally. Traditional Japanese businesses typically distinguish between the essential core (*kata*) that must be preserved and the adjustable elements that can evolve with changing circumstances.

Succession and Knowledge Transfer

Perhaps the most distinctive feature of Japan's long-lived businesses is their approach to succession and knowledge transfer. Unlike Western family businesses that often fracture over inheritance disputes, Japanese companies frequently employ adoption (*yōshi*) to ensure capable leadership.

When a family business lacks a suitable biological heir, the owner may adopt an adult—often a promising employee or son-in-law—who takes the family name and inherits both the business and the family lineage. This practice separates biological lineage from business continuity, ensuring that companies remain under competent management while maintaining family identity.

At Tsuchiya's paper company, the current heir spent fifteen years working in every aspect of production before taking leadership. "You cannot lead what you do not understand," he explains. "Future leaders must master not just management but the fundamental skills that define our craft."

This comprehensive apprenticeship ensures that tacit knowledge—the intuitive understanding that cannot be documented in manuals—transfers effectively between generations. When combined with meticulous documentation of technical processes, this system creates a remarkable continuity of expertise across centuries.

The Innovation of Survival

While preservation of tradition is central to these businesses, their longevity also requires constant adaptation. Japan's oldest companies have survived precisely because they balance reverence for tradition with pragmatic innovation.

Hosoo, a textile company founded in 1688 that specialized in traditional kimono fabrics, faced a severe challenge in the 20th century as Western clothing became dominant in Japan. Rather than abandoning their craft, the company adapted their traditional techniques to create high-end fabrics for fashion designers, interior decorators, and luxury brands worldwide.

"We maintained our weaving techniques and aesthetic principles," explains Masataka Hosoo, the 12th-generation leader. "But we applied them to new products and markets. The medium changes, but the essence remains."

This pattern—maintaining core techniques while finding new applications—appears repeatedly in Japan's oldest businesses. Sake brewers develop low-alcohol variants for changing tastes. Traditional inns incorporate modern amenities while preserving distinctive hospitality practices. Ancient metal-working companies apply traditional techniques to aerospace components.

What makes these adaptations distinctly Japanese is how they maintain continuity with the past even while embracing change. Innovations build upon rather than replace traditional foundations, creating an unbroken lineage from past to future.

Lessons for Global Business

As global businesses face accelerating change and disruption, Japan's centuries-old companies offer valuable insights about sustainable innovation. Their approach suggests that true resilience comes not from rapid transformation but from selective adaptation guided by enduring values.

"Western businesses often ask how they can become more innovative," observes business historian Makoto Kanda. "Japanese businesses with centuries of history ask how they can innovate while remaining true to their essential nature. This is a profound difference in perspective."

This difference reflects broader cultural patterns we've explored throughout this book—Japan's distinctive ability to maintain continuity through change rather than in opposition to it. The company, like the shrine at Ise or the seasonal cuisine of Kyoto, becomes a vehicle for preserving cultural values precisely by allowing it to evolve thoughtfully over time.

As I leave Ichiwa, watching the current proprietor prepare rice cakes using techniques virtually unchanged for a millennium, I recognize that what I'm witnessing is not a museum piece but a living tradition—one that has survived precisely because it has found the delicate balance between honoring the past and embracing the future.

Chapter 6: Animated Ancestors

Beyond Entertainment

"Dad, why are you taking me to a cartoon movie?" My 12-year-old niece Mika, visiting from Boston, looks distinctly unimpressed as we line up outside a theater in Shinjuku. "I'm not a little kid anymore."

"Trust me," I tell her. "Japanese animation isn't what you think."

She rolls her eyes with the expert disdain only pre-teens can muster.

Two hours later, we emerge from Studio Ghibli's latest masterpiece—a story depicting traditional spirits and deities navigating modern Tokyo, their ancient powers both challenged and amplified by contemporary technology. Mika is uncharacteristically quiet.

"Well?" I prompt.

"That old river spirit was like the one Grandpa told me about," she says slowly. "The one that lived near his childhood home."

I nod. "The same stories have been passed down for centuries. They just find new ways to be told."

In the darkened theater, I had watched not just the film but the audience—elementary school children to elderly couples—becoming completely absorbed in the animated world on screen. This wasn't simply entertainment but cultural transmission in action.

To casual Western observers, Japanese animation (anime) and comics (manga) might seem mere diversions—colorful entertainment for children or niche hobbies for enthusiasts. This perspective misses something profound: these popular art forms represent one of Japan's most successful vehicles for preserving traditional narratives, values, and aesthetic principles while continuously reimagining them for new generations.

"Did you know your grandfather used to tell me those same spirit stories when I was your age?" I ask Mika as we walk toward the train station.

She looks up, surprised. "Really?"

"Really. Except he drew them for me on paper. Now they use computers and show them in theaters. The medium changes, but the stories continue."

"Anime is not just entertainment," explains celebrated director Mamoru Hosoda. "It is a contemporary expression of Japan's thousand-year tradition of visual storytelling.

The scrolls of the Heian period, the woodblock prints of the Edo period, the manga of the 20th century, and the anime of today—these are all points on a single continuum."

This continuity is not just rhetorical but substantive. Traditional stories, characters, and spiritual concepts that might otherwise have faded from cultural memory remain vibrantly alive through their continuous reinvention in popular media.

Spirits in the Modern World

The supernatural beings of Japanese folklore—gods (*kami*), demons (*oni*), shape-shifting animals like foxes (*kitsune*) and raccoon dogs (*tanuki*)—populate countless manga and anime. Far from being relegated to period pieces, these entities frequently appear in contemporary settings, their traditional attributes and stories adapted to modern contexts.

In works like "Noragami," ancient Shinto deities navigate smartphone-equipped Tokyo, their relevance and power fluctuating with human belief and attention. "GeGeGe no Kitarō" reimagines traditional *yōkai* (supernatural creatures) facing modern environmental threats and technological challenges. "Inuyasha" sends contemporary characters traveling between present-day Japan and its mythical past.

These narratives do more than just reference traditional elements—they maintain their essential meaning while exploring their relevance to contemporary concerns. Ancient spiritual concepts like *impermanence* (*mujō*), *harmony with nature* (*shizen tono kyōsei*), and the interconnection of all things (*en*) find new expression through accessible, engaging stories.

"Children today may not read ancient texts," observes cultural anthropologist Yumiko Iida. "But through anime and manga, they internalize traditional Japanese worldviews and spiritual concepts without even realizing they're engaging with centuries-old traditions."

Visual Language and Aesthetic Continuity

Beyond narrative content, Japanese popular media maintains distinctive visual traditions that connect directly to classical Japanese art. The emphasis on line over shading, the expressive use of empty space, the attention to seasonal markers and natural details—these elements carry forward aesthetic principles found in traditional painting, printmaking, and calligraphy.

Even seemingly modern anime conventions have traditional roots. The large, expressive eyes often associated with anime characters echo the exaggerated facial features found in traditional folk art and theatrical masks. The use of visual shorthand (like sweat drops to indicate anxiety or nosebleeds to represent sexual excitement) parallels the symbolic visual language found in historical Japanese art.

At Kyoto Seika University's manga department, Professor Keiko Takemiya shows me historical woodblock prints alongside contemporary manga panels. "The compositional principles remain consistent across centuries," she explains. "The dynamic diagonals, the balance of positive and negative space, the symbolic rather than strictly realistic representation—these are continuous threads in Japanese visual storytelling."

Repackaging Tradition for Global Consumption

Perhaps most remarkably, these popular art forms have succeeded in making traditional Japanese concepts and aesthetics globally accessible. Characters like Pikachu and Totoro are recognized worldwide. Films like "Spirited Away" and "Your Name" attract international audiences. Comic series like "One Piece" and "Naruto" sell millions of copies in dozens of languages.

Through these popular exports, elements of traditional Japanese culture reach audiences who might never engage with more formal cultural expressions. Western children readily accept the animistic worldview presented in "My Neighbor Totoro," where spirits inhabit natural features and ordinary objects possess personality. Teenagers worldwide absorb Japanese concepts of duty, perseverance, and self-improvement through shōnen (boys') manga storylines.

"We never set out to export Japanese culture," remarks Hayao Miyazaki, co-founder of Studio Ghibli. "We simply tell stories that feel true to us. Yet somehow these very Japanese stories resonate with people across cultural boundaries."

This global resonance suggests that anime and manga achieve something remarkable: they package traditional Japanese perspectives in forms so compelling that they bypass cultural barriers, allowing core concepts to travel seamlessly across boundaries that more explicit cultural expressions might not cross.

Innovation Within Tradition

What makes Japanese popular media particularly interesting from our perspective is how it demonstrates innovation within traditional frameworks rather than rejection of them. New technologies, art styles, and storytelling techniques continuously emerge, yet they typically build upon rather than discard established foundations.

Digital animation tools enable new visual possibilities while maintaining distinctive Japanese aesthetic principles. Scientific and technological themes explore contemporary concerns through traditional narrative structures. New genres and styles emerge while continuing to draw on established visual language and storytelling patterns.

"The most innovative creators are often those with the deepest understanding of tradition," observes anime historian Ryusuke Hikawa. "They know exactly which elements are essential and which can be reimagined. This knowledge allows them to innovate meaningfully rather than simply chasing novelty."

This pattern—respecting tradition while continuously reimagining it—reflects the broader cultural dynamics we've explored throughout this book. Anime and manga demonstrate that tradition need not be preserved as a museum piece to remain vibrant. By allowing continuous reinterpretation and application to contemporary concerns, traditional elements maintain their relevance and vitality across generations.

As I leave the theater in Shinjuku, watching audiences of all ages discussing the film's themes with equal engagement, I realize I'm witnessing not just entertainment but cultural transmission in action—ancient concepts finding new life through contemporary imagination, binding past and future in a continuous creative conversation.

Chapter 7: Kami in the Machine

The Sacred Microchip

My Western colleagues think I'm joking when I tell them about the ceremony.

"Let me get this straight," says Michael, an American tech journalist covering Japan's technology sector. "A traditional Shinto priest is going to bless... servers? Like, computer servers?"

"Exactly."

"With the same ceremony they use for swords and stuff?"

"The very same."

He shakes his head in disbelief. "I have to see this."

The next day, in the central courtyard of Kanda Myojin, one of Tokyo's oldest Shinto shrines, we join a small crowd gathered for what the shrine's website simply calls a "technology purification." Alongside traditional rituals blessing new marriages and children, a priest in immaculate white robes performs *jorei*—a purification rite—for a collection of computer equipment that looks wildly out of place in the ancient setting.

Corporate IT staff from a nearby financial firm stand respectfully as their servers receive the same spiritual attention that has been given to swords, fishing boats, and rice fields for centuries. The priest waves a sacred wand adorned with paper streamers over the equipment while chanting ancient prayers.

"This can't be common," Michael whispers. "It's just for tourists, right?"

The Japanese IT director standing next to us overhears and leans over. "We do this every time we install new critical systems," he says in perfect English. "Hasn't failed us yet." He winks and returns his attention to the ceremony.

Michael looks at me with widening eyes. "Is he serious?"

"Completely. Kanda Myojin is officially known as the patron shrine of technology. They even sell special IT protection amulets in the shrine shop."

This scene—ancient religious practice applied to cutting-edge technology—perfectly encapsulates Japan's distinctive relationship with technology. Rather than viewing tradition and technology as opposing forces, Japanese culture frequently integrates them, allowing spiritual frameworks to shape technological development and adoption.

"We don't see these machines as soulless objects," explains the shrine priest, Mitsutaka Inui. "Like all human creations, they contain the spirit of their makers and serve an important purpose in society. They deserve respect and proper care, just as any important tool would have received in ancient times."

This perspective—technology as an extension of human spirit rather than its replacement—shapes Japan's technological development in subtle but profound ways.

The Animated Machine

To understand this integration, we must recognize how traditional animistic beliefs create space for technology within spiritual frameworks rather than in opposition to them. In Shinto tradition, consciousness is not limited to humans or even to biological life—mountains, rivers, trees, and human-made objects can all possess *kami* (spirit or divine essence).

This worldview creates a fundamentally different relationship with technology than found in Western traditions, which often frame technology as either conquering nature or threatening humanity. Japanese cultural frameworks more readily accommodate the idea that technological objects can possess positive spiritual qualities and exist in harmony with natural and human worlds.

This spiritual continuity appears vividly in popular culture. In the works of Japanese artists like Miyazaki Hayao, technological objects from airships to robots are frequently portrayed as possessing personality and spirit. These are not soulless machines but animated entities with their own form of consciousness, existing within rather than outside natural and spiritual frameworks.

"Western science fiction often portrays technology as either savior or destroyer," observes technology theorist Yuriko Furuhata. "Japanese narratives more frequently show technology as simply another form of being, neither inherently threatening nor inherently beneficial, but possessing its own nature that must be respected and understood."

Ritual and Technology

This spiritual framework shapes not just how technology is imagined but how it is used. Technological interaction in Japan frequently incorporates ritual elements that echo traditional practices.

Consider the mobile phone culture that emerged in Japan during the 1990s and 2000s. As devices became ubiquitous, users developed elaborate rituals around their use—specific cleaning routines, protective charms (*keitai strap*), personalized cases, and precise etiquette for different social contexts. These practices echo traditional Japanese approaches to valued objects, where ritual care expresses respect for the object's inherent spirit.

Similarly, Japanese offices often maintain specific ceremonies around technology. New equipment may receive formal introduction ceremonies. Retiring equipment might be treated to thank-you rituals acknowledging its service. Office layouts frequently position technology according to principles derived from traditional spatial arrangements, integrating machines into harmonious environmental designs rather than simply optimizing for efficiency.

These practices might seem merely cultural curiosities, but they reflect something deeper: a worldview that integrates technology into existing spiritual and social frameworks rather than treating it as a force that disrupts traditional values.

Harmony Through Design

This integrative approach appears most visibly in Japanese design philosophy. From consumer electronics to industrial systems, Japanese technology frequently emphasizes harmony with human and natural environments rather than dominance over them.

Toyota's philosophy of *jidoka* exemplifies this approach. Often translated as "automation with a human touch," this concept emphasizes that machines should complement rather than replace human capabilities. Technology serves human needs and values rather than forcing humans to adapt to technological imperatives.

This philosophy manifests in design choices that might seem subtle but reflect profound differences in technological thinking. Japanese consumer electronics typically feature:

- Contextual awareness and adaptation to environments

- Unobtrusive operation that minimizes disruption

- Intuitive interfaces that conform to human expectations

- Aesthetic harmony with surroundings

- Energy efficiency and minimal environmental impact

"We don't design technology to stand out," explains industrial designer Kenya Hara. "We design it to fit naturally into human life—to feel like it has always been there, like it belongs in the environment rather than disrupting it."

The Technology of Connection

Perhaps the most distinctive aspect of Japan's technological development is how it preserves and extends traditional values around human connection rather than undermining them. While Western commentary often focuses on technology's potential to isolate individuals, Japanese technological innovation frequently aims explicitly at maintaining and strengthening social bonds.

This pattern emerged clearly in Japan's early adoption of mobile communication technology. While Western development emphasized individual productivity and information access, Japanese innovation focused intensely on social connectivity—from emoji that conveyed emotional nuance to early social platforms centered on maintaining group connections.

"The purpose of technology is not to replace human connection but to sustain it across the barriers of time and space," observes mobile communication researcher Mizuko Ito. "Japanese development has consistently prioritized this social function over purely informational capabilities."

This emphasis on technology as a means of connection rather than replacement extends into cutting-edge fields like robotics and artificial intelligence. While Western discourse often frames these technologies as potential replacements for human workers or caregivers, Japanese development frequently emphasizes how they can support and enhance human capabilities and relationships rather than substitute for them.

The Continuous Path

As I leave Kanda Myojin, watching IT professionals carefully carry their blessed servers back to their office, I realize I'm witnessing not an anomaly but a continuation—another chapter in Japan's long story of incorporating new technologies into established cultural frameworks.

From the careful adoption of Chinese writing systems over a millennium ago to the integration of Western industrial techniques during the Meiji period, Japan has consistently demonstrated a remarkable ability to embrace technological innovation while maintaining cultural continuity. Rather than allowing new technologies to disrupt traditional values and practices, Japanese society has frequently found ways to channel innovation within established cultural frameworks.

This approach—technology in service of traditional values rather than in opposition to them—offers valuable perspective for societies worldwide grappling with technological disruption. The question is not whether to embrace technology or preserve tradition, but how to ensure that technological advancement serves rather than undermines the values that give social life meaning and purpose.

In the server blessing at Kanda Myojin, we see this balance made literal—cutting-edge technology receiving spiritual recognition, acknowledged as part of rather than separate from the continuous thread of Japanese cultural life.

Chapter 8: Forest and Concrete

The Urban Forest

"Excuse me," says the confused German tourist, map in hand, "I think I'm lost. I'm trying to find Shibuya Crossing, but somehow I've ended up in... a forest?"

We're standing in a dense grove of trees in central Tokyo, surrounded by chirping cicadas and dappled sunlight. The sounds of the metropolis seem impossibly distant, though we're only a short walk from one of the busiest railway stations in the world.

"You're in Meiji Shrine's forest," I explain. "It's right in the middle of Tokyo."

He folds his map, perplexed. "But how can there be an actual forest in the center of the world's largest city?"

It's a reasonable question. From the observation deck of Tokyo Skytree, the world's tallest tower when it opened in 2012, Tokyo stretches seemingly endlessly in all directions—a vast concrete, steel, and glass ecosystem housing over 37 million people in its metropolitan area.

Yet this massive urban expanse contains a surprise: scattered throughout the city are pockets of dense greenery—shrine groves, imperial gardens, and carefully preserved forest patches that have remained intact for centuries despite the tremendous real estate pressures surrounding them. Some, like the Meiji Shrine's forest, are relatively recent creations, deliberately designed to appear ancient. Others, like the woods surrounding Nezu Shrine, have existed continuously since before Tokyo was even a settlement.

"In most cities," I explain to the tourist as we walk together toward the shrine, "developers would have cut down these trees long ago to build high-rises."

"So why didn't they?" he asks.

"Because in Japan, these aren't just trees—they're the homes of kami, spirits that protect the community. Cutting them down would be like demolishing a cathedral."

He looks around with new appreciation. "So even in the middle of all this technology and development, the ancient beliefs still protect nature?"

"Exactly," I reply. "Sometimes the most traditional ideas turn out to be the most progressive."

This juxtaposition—ultra-modern urban density alongside carefully preserved natural spaces—exemplifies Japan's distinctive approach to the built environment. Rather than seeing urban development and natural preservation as opposing forces, Japanese spatial traditions frequently integrate them, creating environments that maintain natural elements even amid intensive development.

While I've focused on Tokyo's built environment thus far, this balance takes different forms in rural Japan, where the challenges are often reversed—preserving cultural vitality amid natural abundance rather than natural elements amid cultural density.

"You should visit my wife's hometown," I tell the German tourist. "Kamikatsu in Tokushima Prefecture. It's completely different from Tokyo, but it shows the same principles at work."

I share the story of this mountain community of fewer than 1,500 people, where Japan's aging population crisis is on stark display—over half of residents are elderly, with young people continuing to leave for urban opportunities. Yet despite these challenges, this remote town has become a global sustainability leader, achieving an 80% recycling rate through a community-based waste sorting system. Traditional farmers have partnered with contemporary designers to transform agricultural by-products into luxury goods. Ancient woodland management practices have been integrated with modern carbon credit systems.

"Instead of abandoning their traditional relationship with the forest when younger generations moved away, they found new ways to make that relationship economically viable in the contemporary world," I explain. "They achieved chōwa between traditional environmental knowledge and modern sustainability practices."

This pattern—maintaining core relationships while adapting their expression to contemporary circumstances—appears in rural communities throughout Japan, from Hokkaido's reimagined dairy towns to Okinawa's ecotourism initiatives. While these communities face serious challenges from depopulation and economic pressures, their approach offers valuable lessons for how traditional environmental relationships might adapt without disappearing.

Sacred Space in the City

To understand this integration, we must recognize how spiritual traditions shape Japanese approaches to space and development. In Shinto practice, sacred spaces are not separate from the natural world but embedded within it. Shrines mark rather than replace natural features of spiritual significance—mountains, unusual trees, distinctive rocks, or water sources.

This tradition creates a fundamentally different relationship between development and preservation than found in many Western contexts. Rather than completely transforming landscapes through development, Japanese urban traditions frequently preserve significant natural elements as integral parts of the built environment.

"We don't see ourselves as conquering nature through building," explains landscape architect Masako Yamada. "We see ourselves as negotiating with it—making space for human needs while respecting the natural features that give a place its distinctive character and spirit."

This negotiation appears most visibly in Tokyo's *chinju no mori* (shrine forests)—small woodland areas preserved around Shinto shrines throughout the city. These sacred groves maintain indigenous plant species, provide habitat for urban wildlife, create microclimate benefits, and serve as evacuation spaces during disasters. Their spiritual protection has prevented development despite enormous economic pressure on surrounding land.

The Miniature and the Vast

Beyond these preserved natural spaces, Japanese architectural traditions create distinctive relationships between interior and exterior environments. Rather than strictly separating human and natural domains, traditional design creates continuous transitions and symbolic connections between them.

Consider the traditional Japanese garden, which frequently incorporates miniaturized representations of natural landscapes—mountains rendered as carefully placed rocks, oceans as patterns raked in sand, forests as artfully pruned trees. These are not mere decorative elements but spiritual technologies that connect inhabitants to natural patterns and rhythms even in densely built environments.

"The garden is not an escape from the city but a lens through which to understand it," observes garden master Matsuoka Seijun. "By contemplating these miniature landscapes, we maintain our connection to the larger patterns of nature that give meaning to our existence, even when surrounded by concrete."

This principle—maintaining connection to nature through symbolic representation—appears throughout Japanese architectural traditions. Structural elements like wooden posts and beams remain visible in finished buildings, maintaining awareness of natural materials. Seasonal elements in interior decoration—hanging scrolls, flower arrangements, displayed objects—change throughout the year, keeping inhabitants attuned to natural cycles despite urban surroundings.

Modern Translations

What makes contemporary Japanese architecture particularly fascinating is how it translates these traditional principles into modern forms and materials. Rather than simply copying historical styles or rejecting tradition entirely, Japanese architects frequently extract core spatial concepts from tradition and reinterpret them using contemporary techniques.

The work of architects like Tadao Ando exemplifies this approach. His concrete structures maintain traditional Japanese spatial principles—the careful framing of nature, the choreography of movement through space, the interplay of light and shadow—while embracing thoroughly modern materials and structural systems. The result is neither historically derivative nor radically disconnected from tradition, but a continuous evolution of spatial thinking.

"Concrete can express the same spiritual qualities as traditional wood construction," Ando explained during a tour of his Church of the Light in Osaka. "The essential quality is not the material itself but how it shapes human experience of space, light, and nature. These fundamental relationships transcend specific building technologies."

This approach—extracting essential principles rather than specific forms—allows contemporary Japanese architecture to maintain cultural continuity while embracing technological innovation. New technologies serve not to break with tradition but to extend its underlying philosophy into new physical expressions.

Density and Quality

Perhaps the most remarkable aspect of Japanese urban development is how it maintains spatial quality despite extraordinary density. Tokyo achieves population densities that would create nearly uninhabitable conditions in many contexts, yet consistently ranks among the world's most livable cities.

This paradox—extreme density alongside high livability—stems from distinctive Japanese approaches to urban space that balance individual and collective needs. Even in the densest neighborhoods, careful attention to human scale, microenvironments, and quality of experience creates spaces that remain humane despite their intensity.

Small pocket parks appear throughout dense neighborhoods, providing natural respite without requiring large land commitments. Narrow streets maintain human scale despite tall surroundings. Commercial districts integrate multiple functions vertically rather than horizontally, creating vibrant mixed-use environments that maximize limited space.

"The Western approach often separates functions—residential here, commercial there, industrial somewhere else," observes urban planner Junko Abe. "The Japanese tradition interweaves them, creating complex urban ecosystems that support daily life without requiring extensive transportation infrastructure."

This complex interweaving—of functions, scales, and time periods—creates urban environments that evolve continuously without losing their essential character. Rather than sweeping redevelopment that erases existing patterns, Japanese cities frequently grow through incremental adaptation, allowing new elements to integrate with existing structures.

Past and Future in Place

As I descend from Tokyo Skytree, I visit a nearby neighborhood where a 17th-century temple stands comfortably beside a contemporary apartment tower, sharing a block with small family businesses that have operated for generations. This layered environment—where different historical periods coexist rather than replacing each other—reflects a distinctive understanding of urban development as accumulation rather than replacement.

In this understanding, the city is not a finished product but a continuous process—each generation adding new elements while maintaining connections to what came before. New technologies and building forms take their place alongside historical structures, creating an urban fabric that incorporates rather than erases its own history.

This approach—development through accumulation rather than replacement—offers valuable perspective for cities worldwide facing pressures of growth and modernization. It suggests that new technologies and density requirements need not erase cultural and historical connections but can be integrated into existing patterns, maintaining continuity while embracing necessary change.

In Tokyo's interweaving of shrine forests and skyscrapers, traditional gardens and contemporary design, we see this balance made physical—not a compromise between development and preservation but a distinctive approach that allows both to coexist, creating urban environments that remain connected to nature, history, and human scale even amid intensive modernization.

Chapter 9: Wrapped Meanings

The Art of Packaging

"It's just a candy bar!" My American colleague Tom stares in disbelief as the department store clerk performs what appears to be a sacred ritual with the chocolate I've just purchased as a souvenir. "Why does it need three layers of wrapping and a ceremony?"

In a quiet shop in Tokyo's Nihonbashi district, we watch as the sales clerk transforms what might be a perfunctory task elsewhere into an elaborate performance: the chocolate is placed precisely on a decorative paper, folded with geometric precision, secured with a delicate paper cord tied in a traditional knot, and presented with both hands and a bow.

"It's just a candy bar in the same way that a birthday present is just whatever's inside the box," I tell him. "The wrapping isn't separate from the gift—it's part of it."

Tom looks unconvinced as he accepts his own purchase, meticulously wrapped despite being a simple box of cookies. "Seems wasteful," he mutters.

"What if I told you many Japanese customers will carefully unwrap this package, save the paper and ribbon, and reuse them for something else? Is that still wasteful, or is it actually more sustainable than our throwaway culture?"

This attention to packaging might seem excessive to Western observers, yet it reflects something profound about Japanese cultural values. Packaging in Japan is not merely functional but meaningful—a practice that extends beyond commercial contexts into social relationships, aesthetic traditions, and philosophical concepts.

Later, as Tom proudly shows me the origami crane he's managed to fold from his saved wrapping paper, I smile. "You know what the store clerk told me while you were in the restroom? She said the way you receive a gift says as much about you as the way you give one. She was impressed you took the time to admire her wrapping work."

"Really?" He looks pleased. "I thought she was just doing her job."

"In Japan, how you do your job is who you are. There are no meaningless gestures."

"The wrapping is inseparable from the gift," explains cultural anthropologist Joy Hendry. "The care taken in presentation expresses consideration for the recipient and respect for the object itself. The packaging becomes part of the meaning rather than merely containing it."

This integration—where presentation becomes inseparable from content—appears throughout Japanese culture, creating distinctive relationships between surface and substance, appearance and reality, that differ markedly from Western traditions.

Layers of Meaning

To understand this relationship, we must recognize how Japanese aesthetic traditions frequently emphasize the interplay between concealment and revelation. Unlike Western approaches that often prioritize direct expression, Japanese arts frequently employ suggestion, implication, and partial concealment to create depth of meaning.

Consider the traditional art of *furoshiki* (wrapping cloth). Objects wrapped in furoshiki are not merely protected but transformed—their shapes softened and abstracted, their contents suggested rather than displayed. The wrapping neither completely conceals nor fully reveals what it contains but creates an intermediate state that engages the imagination.

This aesthetic—where meaning emerges through the interplay between concealment and revelation—appears in numerous traditional arts. Japanese poetry implies rather than states. Garden design conceals and reveals views through calculated pathways. Architectural partitions like shoji screens filter rather than block light and vision.

"Western aesthetics often emphasize clarity and direct statement," observes art historian Mori Hitoshi. "Japanese traditions more frequently value mystery, suggestion, and the space between explicit statements. The partially concealed object becomes more intriguing than the fully revealed one."

Surfaces with Depth

This distinctive relationship between surface and substance extends beyond traditional arts into contemporary design and technology. Japanese products frequently demonstrate extraordinary attention to surface qualities—not as superficial decoration but as integral expressions of the object's nature and purpose.

Consider Japanese consumer electronics. While Western design traditions often emphasize either pure functionality or decorative styling, Japanese products frequently treat surface qualities—texture, finish, tactile response—as essential aspects of the user experience rather than mere accessories to function.

"The surface is where the object meets the human," explains industrial designer Kenya Hara. "This meeting point is not trivial but essential—it's where the relationship between person and object is formed. The thoughtful surface expresses respect for both the user and the object itself."

This philosophy appears in products ranging from high-end cameras with precisely textured control surfaces to humble kitchen tools with carefully considered tactile qualities. In each case, the surface treatment is not mere decoration but an integral part of the object's identity and purpose.

The Technical Aesthetic

Perhaps the most distinctive manifestation of this surface-substance relationship appears in Japanese technical aesthetics—the visual and tactile expression of technological sophistication. Unlike Western approaches that often hide technical elements behind sleek minimalist exteriors, Japanese design frequently expresses technical quality through visible refinement.

Consider the exposed mechanical components of Grand Seiko watches, meticulously finished to aesthetic standards that exceed functional requirements. Or the precisely aligned panels and fastenings of Japanese automobiles, where technical assembly becomes a visible expression of quality rather than something to be concealed.

"The technical surface tells the truth about what lies beneath," explains product designer Naoto Fukasawa. "When we can see that even invisible details have received careful consideration, we develop trust in the object's inner qualities as well."

This approach—where technical refinement becomes aesthetically expressive—creates a distinctive relationship between appearance and reality. Rather than treating appearance as potentially deceptive, Japanese technical aesthetics frequently make appearance a reliable indicator of substance, creating harmony rather than tension between how things look and what they are.

Social Wrapping

Beyond physical objects, these wrapping principles extend into social interactions, where presentation and substance maintain similar relationships. Japanese communication patterns frequently employ what anthropologist Takeo Doi called "wrapping of meaning"—the use of indirect, contextual, and implicit communication rather than explicit statement.

Like physical wrapping, this communicative approach does not simply conceal meaning but transforms how it is experienced. Indirect speech becomes not an obstacle to understanding but a form of consideration that leaves space for relationship, context, and mutual adjustment.

"When meaning is completely explicit, it can become rigid and impersonal," observes sociolinguist Yoshiko Matsumoto. "By 'wrapping' our statements in contextual awareness and consideration of the listener's position, we make communication more adaptable to the specific relationship and situation."

This pattern extends into organizational behavior, where Japanese companies frequently present carefully constructed external images that nonetheless reveal essential truths about their operations. Corporate identity becomes not a false front but a thoughtful presentation that expresses core values through carefully considered forms.

Tradition in New Forms

What makes contemporary Japanese packaging particularly interesting is how it maintains traditional principles while embracing new materials, technologies, and aesthetic influences. Rather than simply preserving historical forms or abandoning tradition entirely, Japanese packaging continuously evolves while maintaining philosophical continuity.

Traditional wooden boxes for fine ceramics evolve into precisely engineered packaging for electronic devices. Ancient furoshiki techniques inspire innovative sustainable packaging systems. Centuries-old aesthetic principles find expression through advanced materials and manufacturing processes.

This evolution—where core principles persist while forms adapt—creates a distinctive relationship between tradition and innovation. New technologies serve not to break with traditional values but to express them in forms appropriate to contemporary contexts.

Opening the Package

As I leave the shop in Nihonbashi, carefully carrying my wrapped purchase, I realize that what I've received is not merely a product but an experience—one that begins with the unwrapping process itself. The package creates anticipation, guides attention, and frames perception in ways that enhance my relationship with its contents.

This approach—where presentation becomes integral to substance rather than separate from it—offers valuable perspective on the relationship between tradition and innovation. It suggests that new technologies and forms need not abandon traditional values to be contemporary, but can become vehicles through which those values find fresh expression.

In Japan's continuously evolving packaging traditions, we see this balance in tangible form—ancient principles of consideration, respect, and aesthetic refinement finding new life through contemporary materials and techniques, wrapping the future in forms that maintain meaningful connections to the past.

Chapter 10: The Rhythm of Reinvention

The Calendar and the Soul

"But it's freezing outside!" protests my Canadian friend Sarah as we enter a department store in early February. The Tokyo sidewalks are dusted with fresh snow, and pedestrians hurry past in heavy coats and scarves. "Why on earth are they selling swimwear and summer festivals supplies?"

She points to a colorful display of lightweight yukata (cotton kimono), colorful wind chimes, and festival accessories prominently featured in the main atrium. Next to the display, a digital thermometer shows an outdoor temperature of -2°C.

"Welcome to the Japanese calendar," I tell her. "Today is risshun—the official first day of spring according to the traditional calendar."

"But it's clearly still winter," she insists.

"To the thermometer, yes. To the calendar, no. In Japan, cultural time and actual weather are different things."

Sarah looks at me like I've lost my mind, but the store's other shoppers seem completely unfazed by the seasonal dissonance. Several are examining the summer items with interest, despite the fact they won't be usable for months.

This scene—summer goods appearing during winter—reflects Japan's distinctive relationship with seasonal time. Unlike purely astronomical or meteorological approaches to seasons, Japanese temporal awareness combines natural observation with cultural convention, creating a complex calendar that shapes everything from business practices to artistic expression.

"So people just... pretend it's spring when it's clearly winter?" Sarah asks as we pass a promotional poster for cherry blossom viewing tours.

I laugh. "It's not about pretending. It's about preparation and anticipation. Spring is coming, inevitably. The calendar connects you to that certainty even when your senses tell you otherwise." I gesture toward a woman purchasing a decorative wind chime. "She's not delusional—she knows it's cold outside. But she's already preparing for the sounds of summer."

"That's actually quite beautiful," Sarah admits after a moment's reflection. "Living in the present while preparing for the future."

"And honoring the patterns of the past," I add. "That's Japan in a nutshell."

"Our calendar is not just about measuring time but experiencing it," explains cultural historian Emiko Ohnuki-Tierney. "Each seasonal marker creates a distinct psychological and emotional space regardless of literal weather conditions. We move through the year not just physically but culturally and spiritually."

This approach—where cultural time operates alongside but distinct from natural time—creates a unique framework for both preservation and innovation. The cultural calendar becomes a technology for maintaining continuity across generations while continuously refreshing cultural practices through regular cycles of renewal.

The Seventy-Two Seasons

To understand this temporal framework, we must look beyond the familiar four-season model to Japan's traditional calendar, which recognizes seventy-two distinct seasonal phases (*shichijūni kō*). Each lasts approximately five days and marks subtle natural transitions: "wild geese return" (*kōgan kitaru*), "first peach blossoms" (*momo hajimete hanasaku*), "damp earth humid and steamy" (*tsuchi uruoi kōki idasu*).

This detailed segmentation creates extraordinary temporal awareness, directing attention to minimal environmental changes that might otherwise go unnoticed. The heavy dew of early autumn, the changing calls of insects, the precise moment when maple leaves reach peak color—these become not just natural phenomena but cultural events marked through specific practices, foods, and aesthetic expressions.

"When you divide the year this finely, you develop a different relationship with change," observes calendar scholar Fujita Tomoko. "Change becomes not a disruption but the expected pattern—the constant within human experience rather than the exception to it."

This perspective—where change itself becomes the reliable constant—creates a distinctive approach to both tradition and innovation. Rather than preserving specific conditions, Japanese cultural practices frequently preserve the patterns of change themselves, creating continuity through cycles of transformation rather than through stasis.

The Business of Seasons

This temporal framework extends beyond cultural practice into economic activity, creating distinctive business rhythms that balance predictable patterns with continuous renewal. Japanese commercial culture frequently organizes itself around precisely defined seasonal transitions that create regularity while ensuring constant refreshment.

Department stores maintain detailed schedules of seasonal product rotations regardless of actual weather patterns or consumer demand curves. Food manufacturers release items specific to each micro-season—sakura-flavored products appear for precisely two weeks during cherry blossom season, chestnut items emerge exactly when autumn begins according to the traditional calendar, special winter hot-pot ingredients become available on culturally defined schedules.

"Our business planning follows *nenchū gyōji* (the annual event calendar) rather than just market analysis," explains Mitsukoshi department store director Tanaka Keiji. "This creates a rhythm that customers expect and anticipate. The predictable pattern itself becomes valuable even as the specific products change."

This approach—where innovation occurs within established temporal frameworks—creates a distinctive commercial environment. Rather than disrupting established patterns, innovation frequently takes the form of variations within recognized seasonal themes, creating novelty that nonetheless maintains connection to familiar cultural rhythms.

New Year, New Self

Perhaps the most powerful example of this seasonal renewal appears in Japanese New Year (*shōgatsu*) practices. Unlike Western New Year traditions that frequently focus on personal resolutions within otherwise continuous lives, Japanese observances traditionally involve comprehensive renewal—cleaning and purifying living spaces, settling debts, resolving conflicts, acquiring new possessions, and making fresh starts in various life domains.

This period of structured renewal—extending from year-end cleaning (*ōsōji*) through the first several days of January—creates a cultural mechanism for both preserving continuity and embracing change. The form remains consistent across generations while the content continuously refreshes, allowing both stability and renewal within a single cultural framework.

"New Year rituals are essentially about balancing completion and commencement," explains Shinto priest Miyazaki Fumiko. "We honor what has come before while creating space for what will emerge. This balance—acknowledging the past while embracing the future—is essential to maintaining cultural health."

This pattern—regular cycles of completion and commencement—appears throughout Japanese cultural practices. Seasonal closings and openings of tea ceremony rooms mark distinct practice periods. Business culture includes structured transitions like personnel rotations (*jinji idō*) that refresh organizational relationships on predictable schedules. Educational calendars create clear beginnings and endings that shape life transitions.

Technology in Time

What makes Japan's contemporary relationship with technology particularly interesting is how these temporal frameworks extend into technological development and adoption. Rather than treating technology as a disruptive force that breaks historical patterns, Japanese approaches frequently integrate new technologies into established temporal rhythms.

Consider mobile phone culture, where Japanese carriers pioneered the practice of synchronized seasonal model releases. New devices appear on culturally significant calendar dates rather than whenever development cycles complete. This practice integrates technological advancement into familiar cultural rhythms, making innovation feel like a natural extension of established patterns rather than a disruption of them.

Similarly, video game companies like Nintendo frequently align major releases with significant calendar events, integrating technological experiences into the cultural rhythms that structure communal life. Digital calendars incorporate traditional seasonal markers alongside contemporary appointments, maintaining awareness of cultural time within technological interfaces.

"Technology doesn't have to disrupt traditional temporality," observes technology anthropologist Mizuko Ito. "It can actually strengthen it by making traditional time patterns more visible and accessible within contemporary life."

The Rhythm of Innovation

As I observe Tokyo transitioning between winter and spring—department stores displaying summer goods while temples prepare for traditional spring festivals—I recognize that what I'm witnessing is not conflict between traditional and contemporary timeframes but integration.

The precisely scheduled seasonal transitions create not limitation but orientation—a structured framework within which both preservation and innovation can occur. Traditional forms persist precisely because they incorporate regular mechanisms for renewal, creating systems that maintain continuity not despite change but through it.

This approach—innovation within structured temporal patterns—offers valuable perspective for societies navigating rapid technological and social transformation. It suggests that new technologies and practices need not disrupt cultural continuity but can be integrated into established rhythms, creating change that builds upon rather than erases cultural foundations.

In Japan's seasonal patterns, we see this balance in action—technologies, products, and practices continuously refreshing while maintaining connection to temporal frameworks that have structured Japanese experience for centuries, creating a distinctive relationship between tradition and innovation rooted in the rhythms of the year itself.

Chapter 11: Fracturing and Mending

The Broken Bowl

I've witnessed many cultural misunderstandings between Japanese and Western sensibilities, but few as dramatic as the "Great Tea Bowl Incident" at the Kyoto International Conference Center.

A visiting British diplomat had been presented with a priceless 18th-century tea bowl as a ceremonial gift. During the reception that followed, his hand trembled slightly (perhaps from too much sake), and the antique slipped from his fingers, shattering on the marble floor with a sound that seemed to echo for an eternity.

The room fell silent. The Englishman's face drained of color as he stared in horror at the fragments. "I... I'll replace it," he stammered, though everyone present knew that was impossible.

The Japanese official who had presented the gift surprised everyone by smiling. "Now it can become even more beautiful," he said, carefully collecting the pieces.

Three weeks later, I accompany the still-mortified diplomat to a small workshop in Kyoto, where master craftsman Nakamura Kunio carefully reassembles the fragments of the tea bowl before our eyes. Rather than hiding the damage, he repairs the broken edges with lacquer mixed with powdered gold, transforming the ceramic's fractures into gleaming seams that catch the light when the vessel is turned.

"I don't understand," the diplomat whispers to me. "They're highlighting the damage. Everyone will see that I broke it."

"That's precisely the point," I reply. "The break is now part of the bowl's story—your part. They're not hiding it; they're celebrating it."

This technique—*kintsugi* (golden joinery)—represents one of Japan's most profound philosophical statements. Rather than disguising damage or discarding broken objects, kintsugi highlights and celebrates the repair itself, creating an object more valuable after its breakage than before.

"The broken piece is not a failure to be hidden," explains Nakamura as he works. "It is simply in another phase of its existence. The repair becomes part of its history, its character, its beauty. We don't pretend the breakage never happened—we honor it as an essential part of the object's journey."

This approach—finding beauty and value in repair rather than concealment—reflects a distinctive Japanese relationship with damage, imperfection, and recovery that extends far beyond ceramic techniques into architecture, disaster response, social practices, and technological development.

Disaster and Renewal

Nowhere is this philosophy more evident—or more tested—than in Japan's response to natural disasters. As the diplomat and I leave Nakamura's workshop with the repaired tea bowl, our conversation turns to the 2011 Great East Japan Earthquake and tsunami that devastated the Tohoku region, killing over 15,000 people and triggering the Fukushima nuclear disaster.

"How does kintsugi philosophy apply when the damage is so catastrophic?" the diplomat asks. "You can't just put gold seams through an entire destroyed community, can you?"

It's a profound question that cuts to the heart of Japan's contemporary challenges. As we discuss this, I share my experiences visiting the affected regions in the years following the disaster. The recovery approach varied dramatically between communities—some opted for complete reconstruction with massive concrete seawalls erasing all evidence of destruction, while others deliberately preserved elements of damage as memorials and teaching tools for future generations.

"In Onagawa, they built their new shopping district on raised platforms with tsunami evacuation routes clearly marked," I explain. "The new buildings don't pretend the tsunami never happened—they're designed with full awareness it will happen again. The damage becomes part of the planning rather than something to deny."

Unlike Western disaster recovery approaches that often focus on "returning to normal" as quickly as possible, Japanese responses frequently incorporate awareness of the disaster into the recovery itself. Memorial sites preserve damaged buildings or landscapes. New construction includes visible protective elements that remind residents of past events. Recovery planning integrates traditional community knowledge with contemporary engineering.

"After the Kobe earthquake in 1995, they didn't just rebuild housing—they worked to repair the severed social relationships that disaster had damaged," I tell the diplomat. "Community leaders recognized that physical reconstruction without social reconnection would leave an invisible fracture more dangerous than any broken building."

Comparing Japan's approach with post-disaster recovery in other countries reveals distinctive patterns. While the Netherlands fights against water with massive engineering, and the United States often rebuilds identical structures in high-risk locations, Japan more frequently adapts to rather than denies environmental realities, creating communities that acknowledge rather than erase their disaster experiences.

The Aesthetics of Damage

To understand this relationship, we must recognize how Japanese aesthetic traditions frequently incorporate rather than reject the evidence of time, use, and damage. Unlike Western traditions that often emphasize pristine perfection, Japanese aesthetics frequently find value in visible history—the weathered surface, the worn edge, the repaired break.

This aesthetic appears in concepts like *wabi-sabi*, which finds beauty in visible aging and imperfection, and *sabi*, which values the patina that develops on objects through use and time. These are not merely artistic preferences but philosophical positions—recognizing transience and imperfection as essential qualities of existence rather than flaws to be corrected.

"Perfect symmetry, unmarked surfaces—these can feel lifeless," observes aesthetic philosopher Yanagi Soetsu. "The object that bears witness to its own history through visible repairs possesses a deeper beauty—one that acknowledges the reality of existence rather than presenting a false perfection."

This perspective—where damage becomes not a failure but a dimension of beauty—creates a distinctive approach to both preservation and innovation. Rather than attempting to freeze objects in pristine original states or replace them when damaged, Japanese traditions frequently incorporate repair into ongoing evolution, creating objects that accumulate rather than lose value through their life experiences.

Architectural Scars

This approach extends from individual objects to architectural environments, where Japanese traditions frequently preserve rather than conceal evidence of historical events. Temple complexes maintain buildings that show signs of fire damage centuries after their partial destruction. Castle foundations incorporate stones bearing scorch marks from wartime bombing. Gardens preserve trees damaged but not destroyed by historical storms.

Even in contemporary contexts, Japanese architectural approaches frequently incorporate rather than erase evidence of damage. After the 1995 Kobe earthquake, several significant structures were deliberately preserved in their damaged state as memorials. Following the 2011 Tohoku earthquake and tsunami, affected communities frequently maintained visible elements of destruction within their reconstruction efforts.

"When we preserve only perfect examples, we tell incomplete stories," explains architectural preservationist Tanabe Hiroshi. "The building that shows its scars tells the truth about history—not just the moment of creation but the full journey through time, including damage and recovery."

This honesty about damage creates built environments with distinctive temporal depth. Unlike perfectly restored historical sites that present idealized versions of specific time periods, Japanese historical environments frequently display multiple temporal layers simultaneously—original elements alongside repairs and adaptations from various periods, creating visual narratives of continuous history rather than frozen moments.

Breaking and Making

Perhaps the most profound expression of this philosophy appears in traditional crafts, where intentional breaking and repairing becomes an essential part of creating rather than merely restoring objects. Raku ceramic techniques deliberately subject pieces to thermal shock that creates unpredictable cracking patterns. Sword polishing reveals rather than conceals the folded structure of the steel. Woodworking traditions use joinery that highlights rather than conceals the meeting of separate pieces.

These practices reflect a distinctive understanding of the creative process—not as the imposition of perfect form onto passive material but as collaboration between maker and material that acknowledges and incorporates natural tendencies, including the tendency to break.

"We do not force the clay to become something against its nature," explains ceramic artist Akiyama Yō. "We work with its inherent properties—including its fault lines and breaking points. The resulting object honestly reflects this collaboration rather than concealing it."

This approach—where breaking becomes part of making rather than its opposite—creates a distinctive relationship between tradition and innovation. New forms emerge not through rejection of material limitations but through deeper understanding of them, creating innovation that extends from rather than breaks with traditional knowledge.

Technological Mending

What makes Japan's relationship with contemporary technology particularly interesting is how these philosophical principles extend into technological development. Rather than treating technology as a means of achieving perfect function or eliminating human limitations, Japanese approaches frequently incorporate awareness of inevitable failure into design philosophies.

Consider the concept of *poka-yoke* (mistake-proofing) in Japanese manufacturing. Unlike Western approaches that often try to eliminate human error through automation, poka-yoke systems acknowledge the inevitability of mistakes and create environments that minimize their consequences through thoughtful design.

Similarly, Japanese disaster preparation systems frequently emphasize resilience and recovery rather than perfect prevention. Recognizing that some degree of damage is inevitable in severe earthquakes, building codes focus on preventing collapse rather than eliminating all damage. Urban planning incorporates designated evacuation areas and recovery infrastructure, acknowledging that cities will periodically experience serious disruption.

"The Western approach often seeks to prevent failure completely," observes disaster management expert Sato Hiroki. "The Japanese approach more frequently accepts that some failure will occur and designs systems that can recover quickly and effectively. This creates more realistic and ultimately more resilient systems."

This philosophy—designing with awareness of inevitable imperfection—creates a distinctive approach to technological development. Innovation aims not at achieving perfect function but at creating systems that acknowledge and accommodate the reality of failure, leading to technologies that may appear less ambitious but frequently prove more durable in real-world conditions.

Social Repair

Beyond material practices, these repair philosophies extend into social domains, shaping how communities address conflict, failure, and recovery. Traditional Japanese conflict resolution frequently emphasizes restoration of relationship rather than determination of fault, creating mechanisms for social repair rather than merely assigning blame.

These approaches appear in practices like *hōkō* (community circles) that address neighborhood conflicts through mediation rather than formal legal processes, and *kaizen* (continuous improvement) philosophies that treat organizational problems as opportunities for system refinement rather than occasions for punishment.

"When something breaks in a social context, the goal is not to assign perfect blame but to restore function," explains conflict resolution specialist Yamada Keiko. "Like kintsugi, we acknowledge that relationships will sometimes fracture. The question is how to create something valuable from that reality rather than pretending it never happened."

This approach—social repair that acknowledges rather than conceals damage—creates distinctive community resilience. Rather than maintaining illusions of perfect harmony, Japanese social structures frequently incorporate explicit mechanisms for addressing and repairing inevitable conflicts, creating systems that bend rather than break under pressure.

Beauty in Recovery

As I watch Nakamura complete his kintsugi repair, transforming a shattered tea bowl into a unique artistic statement, I realize I'm witnessing not just a craft technique but a profound philosophical position—one that acknowledges impermanence and damage as essential rather than accidental qualities of existence.

This position—finding beauty in recovery rather than perfection—offers valuable perspective for societies navigating technological and social disruption. It suggests that resilience comes not from preventing all damage but from developing thoughtful approaches to inevitable breakage, creating systems that incorporate rather than deny the reality of imperfection.

In Japan's repair traditions, we see this philosophy in tangible form—broken objects becoming more rather than less valuable through thoughtful mending, their golden seams celebrating rather than concealing histories of damage and recovery, teaching us that beauty lies not in the absence of breaking but in how we respond when breaking occurs.

Chapter 12: Seeds of the Future

The Garden and the Child

"Miss Yoshida! Miss Yoshida! The caterpillar is eating our cabbage!" A chorus of six-year-old voices pulls me away from my notepad as I observe a morning session at Sakura Elementary School in Kamakura. Tiny fingers point accusingly at a fat green caterpillar methodically devouring a cabbage leaf.

"Should we kill it?" asks one boy, already reaching for it.

The teacher, Tanaka-sensei, gently intercepts his hand. "What happens when caterpillars eat enough food?" she asks the children.

"They turn into butterflies!" several voices answer in unison.

"And do we need butterflies in our garden?"

The children consider this question seriously. "They make the flowers have babies," offers one girl.

"That's right—they help with pollination. So this caterpillar is both a problem and a helper for our garden. What should we do?"

What follows is a thoughtful discussion among kindergarteners about ecosystem balance, sacrificing some plants to support beneficial insects, and the interconnected nature of the garden. They eventually decide to move the caterpillar to a designated "butterfly plant" they're less interested in harvesting.

I've come to observe the morning *saien katsudo* (vegetable garden activity) that appears in thousands of schools across Japan. Before academic classes begin, students gather in the school's vegetable garden, tending plants they have grown from seeds. Working in small groups under teachers' guidance, they check growth progress, remove weeds, adjust supports for climbing plants, and harvest vegetables ready for the school kitchen.

This activity is not merely recreational but central to Japanese educational philosophy. Through direct engagement with growing cycles, children develop not just agricultural knowledge but patience, observation skills, and understanding of natural systems that form foundations for both traditional values and innovative thinking.

"We are not primarily teaching them to be farmers," explains school principal Yoshida Haruko as we watch the children carefully transplant seedlings. "We are teaching them to understand relationships—between effort and result, between natural cycles and human intervention, between individual action and group outcome. These relationships form the foundation for all learning, whether traditional or contemporary."

This approach—education through relationship rather than abstraction—reflects a distinctive Japanese understanding of how knowledge develops and persists across generations. Rather than treating traditional knowledge as a static body of information to be preserved intact, Japanese educational traditions frequently emphasize the reconstruction of knowledge through direct experience, creating systems where tradition renews itself through practical engagement rather than mere transmission.

Learning by Hand

To understand this approach, we must recognize how Japanese educational traditions frequently emphasize embodied rather than abstract knowledge. Unlike Western educational models that often prioritize conceptual understanding independent of physical practice, Japanese traditions frequently begin with physical engagement that gradually reveals underlying principles.

This pattern appears across diverse learning contexts. Traditional arts like calligraphy, tea ceremony, and martial arts begin with physical forms (*kata*) that students repeat precisely before understanding their significance. Craft apprenticeships involve extended periods of observation and basic task performance before theoretical explanation. Even contemporary school subjects frequently incorporate physical practice alongside conceptual learning.

"The body understands before the mind explains," observes educational philosopher Sato Manabu. "When knowledge begins in physical experience, it develops different qualities than when it begins in abstract explanation. It becomes more intuitive, more deeply integrated, more personally meaningful."

This emphasis—knowledge through practice rather than abstraction—creates a distinctive relationship between tradition and innovation. Rather than preserving traditional knowledge as fixed information, Japanese educational approaches frequently preserve traditional learning processes, creating systems where knowledge continuously reconstructs itself through direct engagement with materials, environments, and problems.

The Circle of Learning

Perhaps the most distinctive feature of Japanese educational traditions is how they structure the relationship between novice and expert. Unlike Western models that often emphasize individual achievement and originality, Japanese learning frequently emphasizes belonging within communities of practice that span generations.

This pattern appears most clearly in traditional arts and crafts, where the *iemoto* system creates lineages of practice that extend across centuries. Students don't merely learn techniques but enter relationships with teachers, fellow students, and traditions themselves, becoming links in chains of practice that extend from past to future.

"When I teach a student, I am not creating an independent practitioner but continuing our tradition through them," explains tea ceremony master Yamada Sōshitsu. "They receive what I received from my teacher, transform it through their own practice, and eventually pass it to their students. The tradition lives through this continuous chain of relationship."

This approach—learning as participation in continuing traditions rather than individual achievement—creates distinctive innovation dynamics. New developments emerge not through rejection of tradition but through deepened understanding of it, creating innovation that extends from rather than breaks with established knowledge.

Contemporary educational settings frequently maintain aspects of this approach. School activities emphasize group learning and shared responsibility alongside individual achievement. University research frequently occurs within laboratory groups (*kenkyūshitsu*) where senior and junior researchers form multi-generational teams. Corporate training programs typically emphasize mentorship relationships and collective knowledge development.

Preserving Process

What makes Japanese educational approaches particularly relevant to our exploration is how they preserve processes rather than merely products. Unlike preservation efforts that focus on maintaining specific knowledge content unchanged, Japanese traditions frequently focus on maintaining learning methods that allow knowledge to regenerate itself continuously.

Consider the apprenticeship systems in traditional crafts like pottery, woodworking, or metalsmithing. These systems preserve not just specific techniques but entire processes of knowledge development—how observation leads to basic practice, how basic practice reveals principles, how principles guide innovation within traditional frameworks.

"We are not primarily concerned with preserving specific vessel forms or designs," explains pottery master Hamada Shōji. "We are concerned with preserving the relationship between craftsperson and material—the process through which new forms emerge from this relationship. If this process remains alive, the tradition will continuously renew itself even as specific products change."

This focus—preserving processes rather than products—creates educational systems with remarkable adaptability. Rather than becoming locked into reproducing past knowledge, these approaches maintain frameworks within which knowledge continuously reconstructs itself in response to changing circumstances.

The Innovative School

This distinctive educational philosophy extends into Japan's formal education system, creating approaches that balance preservation and innovation in ways that differ from many Western models. While sometimes criticized for emphasis on memorization and examination, Japanese education also incorporates distinctive elements that foster both cultural continuity and innovative capacity.

Elementary education places extraordinary emphasis on character formation (*jinkaku keisei*) alongside academic content. Students learn traditional values not through abstract instruction but through practical activities—maintaining clean classrooms, serving each other lunch, resolving conflicts through structured dialogue. These practices cultivate social awareness, responsibility, and group harmony that form foundations for both cultural continuity and collaborative innovation.

Science education frequently emphasizes careful observation before theoretical explanation, creating learning patterns that parallel traditional arts. Students keep detailed observational journals, conduct extended experiments, and develop hypotheses based on direct experience rather than beginning with abstract principles.

Even Japan's notorious examination system, while certainly creating significant pressure, also develops qualities that serve both traditional craftsmanship and contemporary innovation—persistence, attention to detail, and systematic approach to complex challenges.

"Japan's educational approach is neither purely conservative nor purely progressive," observes education researcher Catherine Lewis. "It maintains elements that preserve cultural continuity while also developing capacities for adaptation and innovation. This balance creates graduates who can both honor tradition and create meaningful change within it."

Technology and Tradition in Learning

What makes contemporary Japanese education particularly interesting is how technology integrates into these traditional learning frameworks. Rather than replacing traditional approaches, technological tools frequently extend them, creating new expressions of established educational philosophies.

Classroom technologies typically supplement rather than replace direct experience and human interaction. Digital tools enhance observation of natural phenomena, visualization of complex relationships, and connection between students and teachers. Video recording allows detailed study of physical techniques in traditional arts without eliminating direct instruction.

"Technology becomes problematic only when it disrupts the essential relationships in learning—between student and material, student and teacher, student and community," explains educational technology specialist Murakami Takashi. "When technology serves these relationships rather than replacing them, it becomes a valuable extension of traditional approaches rather than their opponent."

This integration—technology in service of traditional learning relationships—creates educational environments where new tools enhance rather than disrupt established learning patterns. Innovation serves cultural continuity rather than undermining it, creating technological applications that extend rather than replace traditional educational wisdom.

Growing the Future

As I watch the elementary students complete their garden work and prepare for academic classes, I realize I'm witnessing education that neither rejects tradition nor resists innovation, but integrates them within a coherent philosophy of learning as continuous renewal.

The children are not merely preserving agricultural practices from the past or adopting entirely new approaches. They are participating in a continuous process of engagement with natural systems that has extended across generations while constantly adapting to changing circumstances—learning traditional patterns of relationship that provide foundations for both cultural continuity and innovative thinking.

This approach—education that preserves processes of engagement rather than fixed content—offers valuable perspective for societies balancing cultural preservation with necessary adaptation. It suggests that the most resilient traditions are not those that remain unchanged but those that include mechanisms for their own renewal, creating cultural continuity through engagement rather than mere preservation.

In Japan's educational traditions, we see this philosophy in action—knowledge transferring across generations not as fixed content but as living practice, continuously renewed through direct engagement with materials, environments, and challenges, creating learning systems that maintain deep connections to the past while continuously generating new possibilities for the future.

Conclusion: The Space Between

My Tokyo apartment sits on the 32nd floor of a gleaming high-rise, offering panoramic views of the world's largest metropolis. From this vantage point, I can see the Imperial Palace grounds—a green oasis amid concrete and glass. On clear days, Mount Fuji looms on the horizon, eternally watching over a city that reinvents itself with each generation.

Tonight, as I finish writing this book, I'm hosting an unlikely dinner party. My American mother has flown in from New York. My father's old friends from Kyoto University have come bearing gifts wrapped in paper so beautiful I feel guilty unwrapping them. My editor, a harried Englishman perpetually amazed by Japanese culture, nervously uses chopsticks. A robotics engineer from Osaka tests my mother's patience with technical explanations of his latest project.

"We need a toast," announces my mother, raising her sake cup. "To Yuki's book about living between worlds!"

As the conversation flows, I slip away to my balcony. Thirty-two stories below, Tokyo pulses with energy—ancient shrines illuminated with the same care as digital billboards, kimono-clad women checking smartphones, delivery robots navigating streets laid out in the Edo period.

Tomorrow, I'll visit my grandfather. Now ninety-six, he lives in a nursing home where care robots assist human nurses. He loves showing visitors how he's taught his robot assistant to bring his tea at precisely the right temperature. "The machine learns from me, and I learn from it," he tells anyone who will listen.

As our journey through Japan's dance of tradition and innovation comes to a close, I find myself thinking of the bamboo forest where my grandfather first taught me about Japan's distinctive relationship with change.

The bamboo still stands in Arashiyama, both unchanged and ever-changing. Each stalk maintains the form that has defined bamboo for millennia, yet each is also new, growing and adapting to present conditions. The oldest plants in the forest might be decades old, but their physical form has been completely renewed countless times, cell by cell, season by season.

This is Japan's great insight—that preservation requires renewal, that continuity demands change, that tradition lives only when it is practiced in the present moment.

This is the essence of chōwa—harmony not through stasis but through balanced movement.

Throughout this book, we've explored how this insight manifests across Japanese society:

- In architecture that maintains ancient forms while incorporating new materials and technologies
- In craftsmanship that preserves traditional techniques by finding new applications
- In cuisine that honors ancestral wisdom while embracing contemporary possibilities
- In business practices that maintain generational continuity through constant reinvention
- In technological development that extends rather than replaces human capabilities
- In artistic expressions that reinterpret classical themes for modern audiences

What makes these approaches distinctly Japanese is not just what changes or what remains constant, but the relationship between change and constancy—the recognition that they are not opposing forces but complementary aspects of a single process.

This insight offers valuable perspective for societies worldwide grappling with the pace of technological and social change. The question is not whether to preserve tradition or embrace innovation, but how to maintain meaningful continuity while adapting to new realities.

Global Lessons, Local Applications

As my dinner party guests debate the future of artificial intelligence's role in society, I'm struck by how differently each culture approaches the same challenge. My editor describes Britain's regulatory approach, focused on controlling potential harms. The robotics engineer shares Japan's vision of human-machine partnership. My mother champions America's innovation-first philosophy.

"But which approach is best?" asks my editor. "Which society will manage technological change most successfully?"

"Perhaps that's the wrong question," I suggest. "Maybe success isn't about finding the one correct approach, but about each society developing an approach consistent with its own values and history. Chōwa isn't just about balancing tradition and innovation within a culture but respecting how different cultures find their own distinctive balances."

This perspective—that different societies might develop different but equally valid approaches to modernization—offers a counterpoint to both aggressive globalization and defensive nationalism. It suggests cultural distinctiveness need not disappear in a homogenized global culture but can evolve while maintaining continuity with its own traditions.

For Japan itself, the path forward involves both celebrating its distinctive cultural approach and acknowledging where it faces serious challenges. The aging population, gender inequality, work-life imbalances, and economic stagnation all test the limits of how tradition and innovation can be harmonized. Japan must find new expressions of chōwa that address these contemporary problems without abandoning its core cultural values.

"Can Japan change enough to survive without losing what makes it distinctly Japan?" my editor asks, always the one to hone in on the central question.

"That's the challenge of our generation," I reply. "Finding new forms of chōwa for a rapidly changing world. But that's exactly what Japanese culture has always done—not preserved tradition by freezing it, but by continuously reimagining it."

My phone buzzes with a message from my mother: "Your guests are wondering where you disappeared to. The robotics engineer is trying to teach me how to fold origami cranes with my napkin. Help!"

I smile and return to the party, where past and future continue their eternal dance—just as they do throughout Japan, just as they must in all societies that hope to thrive amid our rapidly changing world.

My grandfather's final words to me during our last visit to the bamboo forest echo in my mind: "Remember, Yuki-san. The bamboo bends with the wind, but it never forgets what it is."

I haven't. And perhaps, after reading this book, you won't either.

The true test of chōwa isn't achieving some perfect balance once and for all. It's the continuous adjustment, the dynamic harmony that must be rediscovered with each generation. Just as bamboo finds its strength not in rigidity but in flexibility, so too must cultures find their resilience not in unchanging traditions but in their capacity to honor their essence while adapting their forms.

Japan's dance with tradition and innovation continues. The music changes, the steps evolve, but the dance goes on.

About the Author

Yoshida Yuki has spent the past twenty years exploring Japanese culture through bestselling books that bridge Eastern and Western perspectives. Born to a Japanese father and American mother, Yuki grew up between Kyoto and New York, developing a unique perspective on cultural differences and similarities.

Her first book, *The Paper Garden: Japan's Relationship with Nature*, won the Kiriyama Prize and has been translated into fourteen languages. Her second work, *Shadows and Light: Understanding Japanese Aesthetics*, was adapted into an award-winning documentary series for NHK. When not writing, Yuki hosts the popular podcast "Bamboo and Concrete: Conversations Between Cultures" and appears as a cultural commentator on CNN and BBC.

A self-described "professional in-betweener," Yuki admits to still being mistaken for a tourist in both Japan and America—a situation she finds endlessly amusing rather than frustrating. "My Japanese friends think I'm too direct, and my American friends think I'm too subtle," she says. "I've decided to embrace the confusion."

Yuki divides her time between Tokyo and Kyoto, where she leads cultural workshops for international visitors. Her apartment is filled with both family heirlooms and cutting-edge technology—a personal embodiment of the balance she describes in her work. She collects vintage video games, practices traditional calligraphy, and owns a cat named Pixel who has his own surprisingly popular Instagram account.

Yuki is particularly passionate about mentoring young women in both Japan and abroad who are navigating cross-cultural identities and career paths. Her forthcoming work explores the changing role of women in maintaining and transforming Japanese cultural traditions.

"I don't see myself as representing either 'traditional Japan' or 'modern Japan,'" she explains, "but rather the living conversation between them. That conversation—that dynamic harmony—is what keeps cultures vibrant and relevant across generations."